TRUTH IN A SEA OF OBFUSCATION

By Christopher Moors

ISBN-10: 0985697938
ISBN-13: 978-0-9856979-3-8

Published 2010 by the Creative Cosmos

Printed in the United States of America

Dedicated to True Spiritual Warriors

Showing courage to move towards the new,
Cultivating integrity to make choices for good,
Demonstrating creativity in every aspect of life,

You are the heroes of Future Humanity.

Table of Contents

Table of Contents

To the Earth We Go

"To the Earth we go," we said upon entering this solar system. Diving into the time portal and undertaking the compression of incarnation, we temporarily lost our memory. Connecting to the soul, we easily remember our past and have glimpses into our future. Resist not and all shall be revealed. One constantly loses energy by denying parts of themselves that need to weep and/or mourn. Lazarus was raised from the dead through tears. The ache of the heart was so great and the power of forgiveness so transcendent that resurrection spontaneously resulted.

Sometimes we focus on one event and there is another that brings the deeper meaning. The symbols in your life are like one big tarot card spread telling you a story right out in the open if you can read it. Each relationship reflects some aspect of your inner self. Every planetary conjunction begets manifestations that can beguile the very soul. Indeed, there is no easy trail leading out of here. Repent ye and walk back the path ye came. This is the road home to peace, fulfillment, and at long last a good rest. Every time you fall along the way, get back up and walk on.

Whenever you hear the pitter patter of rain or see the sun dancing upon the ocean, remember Me. Not me in a writer's body but Me in every body. It is always Me trying to communicate to you. So many imperfect yet beautiful mediums trying so hard to serve Me. I am truly blessed to be/meet you. For certain if you come across these words, it is for the purpose of Me reaching Me in You. If I can pull Me out then You will be Me/free too. Manifestations of Me, namely You, will have a variety of lexicons and frames of reference and that creates a beautiful tapestry.

There is a big difference between dabbling in the occult and actually being on a self-disciplined path of enlightenment. Some with the first taste of the 4th dimension go mad with self-righteousness and let pride devour their piety. You may remember your past lives, open your energy centers, astral project/lucid dream, learn to use psychic abilities and get all kinds of communications from entities on the other side, but this does not mean that you are fully awakened. In fact it is more likely than not that you will be lost into the thorns of wielding a small amount of power.

Beware the words of the so-called wise. Sometimes a bit of the truth mixed with conjecture can lead you farther astray that none at all. Take what you read or hear as something to be considered not believed in. If someone insists then move away fast. They are trying to steal your freedom and use you to their own end. A true friend will respect your individual autonomy without you having to ask. Pleasant will be the feeling of mutual understanding and sharing that takes place amidst a backdrop of gratitude. Love expands, control contracts, and peace is bliss.

Truth in a Sea of Obfuscation

Many people tremble when the occult is brought up. It immediately challenges old belief systems to have a simple conversation on metaphysics. This society is already thin on art and music education, but if you consider the heavenly nature of humanity, there is a shocking shortage of true centers of divinity. Generations of kids have come and gone without knowing the first thing about auras, chakras, or meditation. These things have been known and taught in many world cultures. The knowledge has been kept alive by daring sages through the ages who sacrificed their all to preserve the truth in a sea of obfuscation.

The church is the default filler of the community void, but what to do if you do not believe in it? One should not accept a religion just because their circumstance was such that they were born in it. Everybody should question everything and tenaciously too! Others may feel uncomfortable, but it is in fact an imposition on you if you are pressured not to speak of these topics. Perhaps Jesus is not the only way. There are many great lessons in the spiritual traditions of the Earth. There are no chosen people as all are holy.

We need cosmic community centers with open information portals. It is ludicrous to limit your research to one book.

Tap your neighbor on the shoulder and quietly inform them of the conspiracy to enslave humanity. Bring up in 'good company' that the Federal Reserve is a private bank that prints money out of thin air and loans it to you with interest. Keep your sensory portals open so you can negotiate the astral road of angels, demons, and souls. There are a plethora of entities trying to influence perception both on the outer and inner planes. This is why it is so essential to withdraw at times to the inner temple and sacred aloneness of your heart. Stillness and calm restores the space that answers all questions before they are even asked.

It is tiring to see the same old stories sold again and again. Zen is not like this in any way. Zen is not like anything. Zen has Zest and is Zany. If Americans could become more aware of this real freedom they wouldn't be such easy prey for slogans. Just think of all things you are practically forced to recognize. Take the Tyranny of the Holiday for instance. Every year on the same day you are expected to do the same thing. This is thoroughly integrated with the country's economy and it is assumed that it will last in perpetuity. Try dropping out and see how hard they fight to bring you back in. All of this takes place on a mental plane that can be transcended with awareness. Your own truth is in a higher place. The sun rises and sets on each day fresh and clean.

The trees do not believe in a Monday.

You Might Hear an Angel Call Your Name

Hello my dear stranger/friend. Welcome to this area of the Universe. If you are reading this you have chosen to take the risk of incarnating on Earth. You have allowed yourself to forget where you have come from in order to have this experience. Remembering is possible. The most important technique to learn is to stay in one place. Running around we stir up so many things that to see clearly through the fog is impossible. If we sit still, things settle. If we choose to not go on the ride of our emotional whims, we begin mastery.

The outer characters will draw you into their play if you let them. It is best to dance in and dance out…play around the edges of this world. See the things of value. You have come here with a unique mission necessary for the evolution of the species. There is nobody else who can do what you came here to do. You will know you are on the right track when every body else tells you that you are wrong. *"Conform you silly goose!"* No no no…let the creativity spill out. Yes yes yes…now the flow is happening. Forge a new path.

Drawing from inspiration we paint tapestries of dreams. It is a miracle that we can participate in the experience first hand. Suspended in space we pass the time. Like bees full of honey, we share our bounty to the benefit of the community. Through struggle or peace we tell each other tall tales and shape our reality accordingly. There are as many different versions of this story as there are entities telling it. Throw a couple of sentient beings in a room and soon they'll be comparing notes, making deals, and procreating if possible.

Swirling vortexes take us from one dimension to the next. Parallel realities exist simultaneously with this one and occasionally bleed over. We all make many mistakes before we get things right. There is no condemnation for what is intrinsic to the circumstance. There is music running through it all, tying everything together. There is romance between life and life in celebration of life. Swaying and swerving; swooning and curving, we let loose our energy in a myriad of forms and poses…yoga from the inside out.

Listen closely and you might hear an angel call your name. They will whisper it softly in your astral ear. Listen closely and you might hear an angel call your name. Simply and sweetly like a melodious tune. Listen closely and you might hear an angel call your name.

They are there waiting for an invitation. Listen closely and you might hear an angel call your name. They are with all of your friends and loved ones on the other side. Listen closely and you might hear an angel call your name. Just before sleep and when you awake.

Universal Consciousness in Every Particle of Existence

Creatures in thousands of varieties populate the Universe. How sad to believe in dirt amidst a garden of dreams. The oscillation of history's events proves repeatedly that when offered the chance to deceive many will.

Animals as you know them now will no longer remain on Earth if there is not a major diversion from the current course. One day, stories of them will be doubted by the majority of remaining humans as ancient myths of a primitive people.

There are many examples of animals speaking in clear human language. With the Universal Consciousness anything is possible. The eye looking back at you has seen much in many forms and traveled very far.

Some of the dinosaurs died and some moved on. Many never left the astral realms. They are not available to the highest wisdom until they incarnate as mammalians. There is a subset of the species that refuses to make this leap.

Try not to think too hard because it will block the remembrance that supercedes such dense gyrations. OUT THERE is not nearly as vast as IN HERE. OUT THERE is IN HERE but the reverse is not true. No filters; no interpretations.

Aware of the 'I' and the 'Super I', the wanderer sets off in search of dispersion into all things. The connection is the vibration within every particle of Existence. Your chair can tell you the truth if you coax it hard enough.

Begging for bits we nibble nimbly. Shouting for enlightenment we provoke the lightning to strike our heart. Foolish devils try to beguile with a sly smile. They will meet their own Armageddon on the killing fields of humanity.

Joy and Pain Will Cleanse our Soul

Dare I go too far once more mocking/unlocking the foundations of reality? Sights, sounds, smells, touches, and tastes, shall fool/rule no longer. Decoding the external world, and giving an imprint in the brain to help us relate, they are not what they seem to be. Atoms can take on many forms. With inspiration, they bend to the will of One.

Dragging our bodies around we sometimes stumble upon a moment of grace. At once amazing and beneficent, the ringing of cosmic music whimsically whistles through the trees. We are being constantly coaxed to another way. Harmony can abide and peace will prevail. The burden lifts and through the clouds we see the reason behind it all.

The tumult of prayer at the expense of others creates much noise in the astral realms causing manifestations to be skewed. Wishing earnestly is not as effective as nurturing nature. Good grapes can only come from a healthy vine. Withering are those that seek to be other than what they are and fall disappointed when the impossible never happens.

It is a wonder how our energy attracts to us exactly what we need at any given time. Sometimes the RANDOM VARIABLE enters into our lives and starts to wreak havoc. This is when survival depends on strength and a never give in/up approach. There is no failure. We must adjust and persevere. Knock on every door once, twice, or thrice.

Beauty is what happens when body is illuminated by soul. A scarred/scared hunk of flesh can be attractive if the light of love is within. Humorous are the minions when they are abuzz with intrigue. Who is doing what and with whom? Outer and inner begin miles apart. When they merge into a synergistic whole the curtain comes down on the act.

DNA is like a billion keyed piano. All we need to play better tunes are more fingers. Press the right button and anything can happen. Soon humanity will be building new creatures from the ground up. In the underground cities these beings already exist. Scientists are free from restriction down there just as long as they keep coming up with weapons.

We'll all face our own demise sooner or later. The question will be how we face it when it comes. Hopefully I'll be able to jump right out of the body into an astral landscape populated with family and friends. Reunions and getting acclimated to the new environment will alternate with visits to those who are left behind. Tears of joy and pain cleanse our soul.

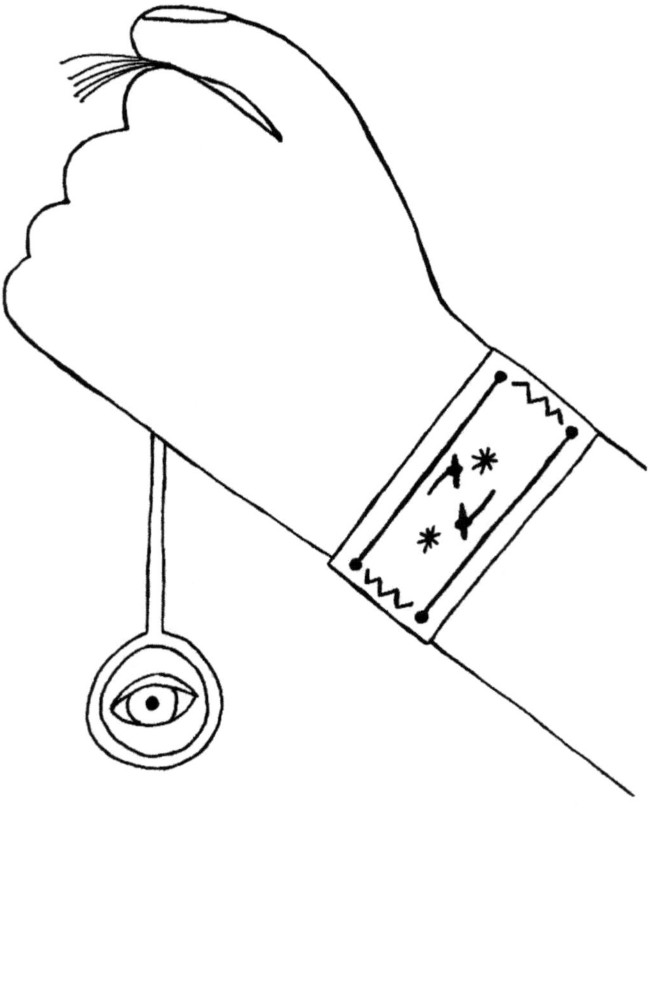

A Place in Space that Happens through Time

We live and operate on a plethora of levels simultaneously; we are many and we are one.

Whatever we come up with creatively has to already be there in the fabric of the Universe as part of the subset of possibilities. That is why it is not very helpful to claim the creation as property and something that is "mine". Sharing thoughts and ideas freely, you can become a vortex of synergy through which the spirit can be invigorated and seek out the audience necessary for the messages capable of being conveyed through the willing facilitator. It is a tricky practice to keep the personification in the body from contaminating the divine discourse. That is why it is essential to let all information come in and go out smoothly. Whatever is truth for you will have the necessary impact on its own. There is no need to hold on to the data. This will only use up energy and wear you out.

In the past at different times in various situations an individual would become awakened and students would gather around to receive the fruits of his/her realization. In the modern era with all knowledge from all history available at our fingertips and new insight being added by many people all the time, there is no need to become fixated on anyone or anything. There are as many paths as there are humans walking them. Gathering wisdom from every tradition our practice is enriched. The unity of truth reveals itself as we transcend to a place where we understand it is simply the language being used that varies as per the audience and the given era of transmission. Cross referencing traditions produces a solid model from which we can draw in the search for our own enlightenment.

Expressing as you gain experience allows the potentialities to become manifest and clears out the inner world to make room for new influxes of energy from higher sources. Leaving no stone unturned, we shine light on every last corner of our subconscious. As we go deeper it will get more painful. The universe might send the right friend at the right time to tell us exactly what we need to hear, but if we are unable to receive the message the concept will still be lost. It is important to remember that although we may see people as an 'other', in fact they are us and we are they. There is no distance between us existentially. Even our enemies can be friends if we look at it from the right perspective. We will never lose our humanity with its complexity; we can gain our divinity with its blessings.

These intricate interplays happen on the micro interpersonal level and the macro international level. Are not "terrorists" trying to bring something to our attention? If we call them evil and negate everything they say we remain in denial and fail to learn the lessons contained within the scenario. Often it is our hypocrisy that results in part of our soul either as a person or nation being cut off and left to die. This then draws to us the attention getter that attempts to break through the China wall that protects this wound. Often instead of opening to healing we declare war and try to destroy the perceived opposition. At the end of the war the two parties are forever intertwined anyway. Keeping the channels of communication open is of complete necessity. This is the importance of diplomacy for nations.

It is not up to any one of us to save the world; it is up to each of us to do what we can.

Cosmic Drama Winds Ever On

Whatever the season in the land of humanity, the individual can rise in consciousness. The outer only infringes on the inner if you let it in. Establishing a solid core beyond the world allows you a freedom that can not be found in externals. The symbol of the eye represents the watchful state of awareness at rest within itself. Pooling energy, nothing is wasted on unnecessary thoughts and actions. There is no need to rush because artificial time considerations are no longer superimposed.

When the heart opens, music connects you to all of existence. You notice now that nature was always trying to get your attention. Who do the birds sing for but for you? Sure they might sing for the Sun, but they need an ear closer to the ground to maximize their purpose, for every heart moved by the beauty of the song compounds its blessing. Do not the Lilly's of the valley make you smile? An eagle soaring overhead will always inspire awe and admiration. A flowing river begets silence.

No matter how trying the time, it will not last forever. However this message finds your mood or attitude know that if you are struggling in any way, there is hope. Everything experienced is a lesson to learn. Inevitably things will loosen up. There can not be a down without an up. Balance through non-attachment is the ultimate as the ups and downs no longer hold sway over the individual's state of being. Whatever 'is', is accepted and used to supplement the meditative practice.

Never let the dark side swallow you up and close you in on yourself. Too many people get caught in never ending thought loops that destroy their capacity to act in a creative or productive way. If someone from the outside tries to assist it may then be seen as a threat and guarded against as opposed to them letting help in. It will take a major occurrence to get past the resistance once it gets to this point. A total reevaluation from the inside out will have to be provoked in order to free the talons of this beast.

Sweet relief is found when that which can not be controlled is let go. The world will go on its way; the story continues to be written. No matter how smug the mug on the boob tube, no one knows what will happen tomorrow, or even 5 minutes from now. The Earth is a stage and the play is being composed on the fly. The actors on Broadway are participating in a play within a play. Imagine if they wrote and performed a play about a play! The Cosmic drama we all are stars in winds ever on.

A Blessing Beyond Compare

Consciousness is the ultimate goal of incarnation on Earth. Evolution has produced the perfect 3D body, and now spirit can become self-aware through this vehicle. It is a long process when measured in time but seen outside of these parameters, it is a near instant manifestation. All troubles and stresses dissolve in the light of transcendent presence. Opening our mind and healing our emotional wounds, we make room for our higher self to merge with the personal identity we use to relate in the confines of this environment.

Gaining more and more knowledge will not bring us the freedom we seek. It may well confuse us further as contradictions mount and we bump into the limits of our bio-computer's capacity. Our soul has no such limits. Containing our epic history and experience accrued from many lifetimes, we have to get over our body-persona to access these treasures. We are not who our neighbors believe us to be, and this constant reinforcement of our 'I' should be understood as nothing but a mechanism for communication.

The mental plane is where we store information, and it is also the place through which entities on the astral realm imprint us with their messages. The trick to deriving the meaning is tracing the imagery back to its source and not doubting what your intuition is revealing to be the truth. Sometimes what we find out is fantastic or near unbelievable, but so is our life here in the first place. There can be no greater miracle than that which is occurring already every minute of every day.

It is a blessing beyond compare to have friends and loved ones to share this bizarre and wonderful celebration with. Sure there are plenty of badies around that try to spoil the dream and sometimes they can come very close to doing so. Take heart, because the universe will never let the darkness become permanent. Intrinsic to the very fabric of existence is our inevitable success. That which is potential will one day become actual, through us, and peace will follow as its shadow.

To Forgive is Truly Divine

There are so many variables and mixed messages flying around that you can be quite certain that there is not one person who has a clear vision of what needs to be done in the grander scheme of things. That is fine because it is not a necessity. The important thing is for the individual to do well in their environment and bring forth their innate potential. If everybody does this, the grander scheme takes care of itself.

Some say humanity will awaken very soon and some say it will take 1000 more years. Either way it hardly matters since time is an illusion. The sun rises and sets and people give the appearance of aging. With a little DNA tinkering this too will probably be a thing of the past. You'll be able to go to the lung shop and get another pair just like you do when your shoes get worn out. They will be new and improved!

Are there people trying to manipulate and control things? Yes, but not to the extent that they would like you to believe. The danger of getting carried away with the conspiracy theories is that at some point you start empowering the conspiracy. People get so worked up they think Big Bro is behind every communication. George W. is hiding in your underwear drawer and wants to know why it is not in order.

There is no other person that knows the mysteries of your inner world. It is a miracle that we get along with each other as well as we do. Friendliness towards others begets friendliness towards your self. So many things in the Universe work with this reflexive property. If you think the world is out to get you, be assured that for you it is. If you think that doors of opportunity are going to easily open, they will.

Ask by focusing your intent and it shall be given as a manifestation of your own Will. You must meet the Universe halfway by planting the seeds of success. Each conscious act will bring an abundant return. Being an island unto oneself is a guaranteed way to dry up and die. We need each other no matter how scary it is to trust. Somebody might hurt you, but still we must learn to love in many situations.

Freedom from being reactive is the best gift you can give yourself these days. When you are with others, be respectful enough not to project your past wounds onto them and react as if they are doing what you fear. There is so much psychological damage in the populace that we have to be gentle and helpful as much of the time as possible. To forgive even if an error is not acknowledged is truly divine.

The Universe has anticipated your Needs

There are many forces blowing like winds through the astral realms. At any time a human can open to one of these forces and allow it to possess them and use them as a vehicle for expression. Anger runs through people, one to the next until it comes up against someone who has learned enough self-control not to react. Any of these individuals under the influence of anger can be considered demonic for as long as they are under its sway. That is why it is important to proactively maintain your aura.

It is good to be open and trusting to others; it is important not to overextend yourself. Awareness must shine like a sun from your core. Steady and unwavering, the diligent monk offers friendship and can't be hurt because he understands the situation too well. Any betrayal of his trust is more harmful to the betrayer than he. For the monk, life goes on and friendship is extended to the next person with no hesitation due to the preceding occurrence. Transcending association, each individual is treated like the first.

Other forces are more benevolent in nature such as love, laughter, and seeking knowledge. In fact every person, planet, star, or god that has ever existed can be tuned into like a frequency. An adept facilitator can reside in their own soul and read another's soul, giving them insight into their friend's destiny. Sometimes someone's higher self will compel them into the presence of a psychically inclined person in order to tell their own physical self something of great importance. Usually, "Keep on moving!"

We evoke a force when we present a symbol. I use the Aum and Yin Yang because they represent all pervasive Universal Vibration/Presence and Harmony/Balance/Awareness. Opening to these invigorating influences, I stay immersed so I never forget. Existence itself can use you to deliver divine discourses. More than once people have expressed to me how timely certain messages have been for them. The Universe has anticipated the moment you will need/read it and flowed toward you through me.

One of my favorite Zen sayings expresses that in the end, rivers will be rivers again and mountains will be mountains. This has always stayed with me because it is simple and profound. It has spoken to me in different ways at different times. One of the things I realized (which shouldn't be said) is that when we first become aware of ourselves as life on planet Earth, everything is stirred up on many new levels. We are amazed with the astral world and it colors what we see. When it too settles we can enjoy the obvious.

Vibes from the Cosmic Computer

Humans are relatively new to the planet Earth. Quickly you have dominated the globe. Some years ago you used to be peaceful half-monkeys, but then the greys came. They tinkered with your DNA and now you are self-conscious but tortured. In your old state you were at peace but ignorant. As you are now you have not yet arrived.

Part of the grey's reason for facilitating the rise of the new humanity is so that the bodies grown on Earth could host the variety of alien intelligences incarnating there. Star travelers from Orion, Sirius, Arcturus, Aldebaran, Pleiadies, and all the usual local Milky Way galaxy suspects currently exist simultaneously on the planet.

About 1/3 of the humans are terrestrials; souls that actually were born on planet Earth. Sometimes these young souls get overwhelmed with the circumstances they face. It is likely that they haven't attained the subtle consciousness yet. They are prone to primal wounds and high levels of denial. They are sweet but naive.

What you call bacteria and viruses are actually supremely intelligent beings that are constantly in contact with one another. Their form might be simple, but the focused resonance is actually very high. They exist on different dimensions, which is why they have such a harmful effect when they come into contact with the body suits. They can never touch your essence, but they disrupt dense vibrations.

Mythos of your Soul

There are those amongst us who criticize the old religions and rightly so. But many times they instead create a Hyper-Morality and wrap themselves in it. Of course the limiting beliefs of old are easy to digest, dissect, and render back to their proper place as a creative work of humanity trying to come to terms with itself within a given era. The Hyper-Moralist is complex, full of self-justifications and judgments of superiority. He is much farther off of Tao than is a person with simple honest faith. This is one of the many and challenging pitfalls as we head toward greater awareness.

The goal is to recover who we truly are. Nothing is needed from the outside. There is obfuscation in the density of the 3rd dimension. It is a compression pushing down on us and causing us to forget. We get forced out through the senses and tricked into believing what we see there. In the jungle there are many traps. Hell is falling in to one and forgetting how to get out. We might resist, but sometimes a strong helping hand is just what we need. The question is whether the Ego can get over itself long enough to accept this help. Blessed are they who give *and* receive.

Truth is self-evident and lives in your heart moment to moment. You live Christ-like, or in Buddha-hood. You are the mythos that ignites wonder in the depths of your soul. The smile that comes from peace shines brighter than the sun. Know that though the society presents many challenges, the whole opportunity is a miracle. What are you doing here if you didn't choose to be? Did God enslave you to the whims of fate? There is dignity in the successful struggle towards maturity and wisdom. You can recognize those who have understood when they remind you to think for yourself.

Our Divine Heritage and the Astral Deity Hierarchy

Consider this for a moment. Though you may feel as if the ground is solid beneath your feet.... Though you may think you see what seems to be outside of you... Though even now you can hold your hands out in front of your eyes... It is all simply a vibrating flux being processed in your mind. And as we clearly know, this perception is but an infinitesimally small slice of factors at play in the universe.

The world moves in the wake of your intention. People and events on the outside accurately represent the state of being inside. Your friends are like a living tarot deck giving you hidden indicators about yourself. Messages are around you all the time decoding events. Numbers, animals, stars, dreams, synchronicity.... Everything is telling you exactly what you need to know now right out in the open.

The terrifying truth that we are immersed in all of this worldly commotion to avoid is our innate aloneness. This is a burning realization and also the doorway to our soul quality uniqueness. We can never fill the emptiness of want with external sensation. It must be filled with inner light to be satiated. When we create, the fires start burning and the rivers start flowing. Ice starts melting and the spring comes.

The Holy Spirit enters through the passageway of the medulla oblongata. It lights up the brain and gazes through the eyes of the willing vessel. The individual is still there and is now illuminated with a guiding presence that eases pain and supersedes definition. There is a friendly quality about it...a hallowed sacredness with a good nature and bubbling sense of humor. There is a coaxing to join the celebration.

The strength of your Will comes from your father who art in the heavens, the Sun, or as I like to call Him Sol. This Lord of the Heavens (also Ra) is a local god and not the Oneness within all things which is the Source/Tao/Aum. This transcendent Source has created many suns/sons. These suns/sons have married planets to create living children of their own. When these children have their own children, the sons/suns of Source become a grandparent and the Source itself becomes a great grandparent.

In this way we all have a divine heritage. Many of us have gone through this process in other places with other sons/suns of God/Source. There are many here from the Pleiades. There are some from Sirius, Andromeda, Orion's belt, and representatives from dozens more. We all simply take a body to live on planet Earth. There are also mythological entities, Satyrs, Trolls, Fairies, and Elves in human bodies now. Not to mention Earth animals who have worked their way up in consciousness. Often dogs, cats, and owls are among the first to make the leap.

To jumpstart the spiritual evolutionary process some on Earth have taken Magic Mushrooms, also known as psilocybin. These eye openers are a gift from an ancient race of space travelers. They used to visit Minerva (the asteroid belt planet), but stopped coming to this solar system after what happened to Mars. They left their DNA awakening gift under trees on Earth so that they might still be contacted telepathically. They no longer take physical bodies and exist only as a specific frequency in the upper echelons of the astral deity hierarchy.

Shockingly Tremendous Zen Awakening

You have to accept illusory parameters to witness illusory events. This hunk of meat we are running around with processes information in a way that makes the physical world seem real. We can eat a sandwich, smoke a joint, and make sweet Love; those are some of the big reasons we come back here. Something in our psyche becomes addicted to the sensation of the garden's pleasures. We want more and more and more of this experience. Orbiting the Earth, our Souls take bodies again and again to facilitate this need. Everything we desire is a drug that holds our freedom in its existence.

Stop the mind for a moment and focus on the slippery-ness of our situation. Some bodies that come to the Earth die at birth. Some barely live a couple of years. Others are taken in accidents along the way or get struck with a debilitating illness. If you are a healthy adult human, consider it a miracle that you are here and be extremely grateful. It is one of the rarest things in the Universe. This precious time is now available for attaining consciousness. Blooming even once is enough to change the whole Cosmos forever.

We are all One and are happy that you've come upon this essay as it might help.

Lay down your normal mode of perceiving and let it lift into higher vibrations. Outside of the senses is where all the mega realizations lie. There is such a thing as the shockingly tremendous Zen awakening. There is a deeper Source of Life that will light you up like a human body bulb. Then your aura will shine so bright it will be undeniable. That is why the old Zen masters were always able to recognize when the disciples became enlightened. There is no hiding it! The glimmer in your eye will give you away. You will be trying to keep from laughing but will be unsuccessful.

Even now this ending is beginning. All things are occurring simultaneously in living principle. Equations of love are darting across space leaving trails of dreams. Broken hearts litter the landscape and the echo of their pain still rings amongst the stars. Rainbows of light heal the soul with reunion, resurrection, and hope. The emotional water based nature of this place makes it excellent for probing the deepest mysteries of the galaxy. There is a truly much grander perspective than what we are fed in the mass media. Take all the pieces, put them together, and throw them away.

Every time a word takes form it comes from the invisible. All *something* comes from *nothing*. *Nothing* has infinite capacity and endless ingenuity. One of my greatest visions was of flying up and out of here, looking back, putting it all in a ball and knowing that behind it all was *nothing*. Speechless with a tear in my eye, I wandered in a daze for days. Then the sudden balance of the opposites, the uncoiling of the kundalini, the opening of psychic perception, and the downloading of past lives. Of course if you're lucky enough to make it this far you can rejoin your greater soul journey.

Make Your Own Connection to the Source

Blessings flow and like attracts like; harmony abounds. Seek not and all is found. The present is an eternal flux that cuts through time like a blazing sword through tofu. Make sure you add plenty of spices to maximize flavor. It is not sinful to delight in abundance. What a wonderful thing to share this multitude of favors. Health is a gift and all else is gravy. It would be a sad thing indeed to waste the opportunity to make friends and create beauty.

Many in despair might falsely believe that they would give up this life. Countless stories have been told of someone seeking to end it all regretting the choice in the last moment. They do so because the contrast of death brings life into focus. It becomes clear how precious and delicate is this transitory happening. At the core of Zen is this remembrance. The end is always nigh. Very soon it will be over. Take the chance to dance.

A rose by any other name might be just as sweet, but a rose without a name has another level of luster. An experience without preconception is fresh and new. Coming into something attempting to conform reality to your tiny terms is like sailing a tugboat into a typhoon. Whatever we do, take solace in the fact that it was part of the inherent set of possibilities or else it couldn't have been done. What the hell kind of crazy experiment is this anyway?

Come to Earth, make Love and have it all torn away. The only way it makes any sense is that eventually we will be let in on the gag. Just like fraternity hazing, God is kicking our butt. When we establish acceptance for that which is, and cease to believe so absolutely in the physical reality which can be scientifically proven not to be there, we begin to loosen up on the whole thing and are more able to make our own connection to the Source.

There is no reason to get overly serious about self and the implications thereof. A cosmic accident with an eye on the prize, humanity is abuzz with gossip. Looking at each other they wonder why they see not themselves. Yanking the speck out of their brother's eye, they are constantly knocking planks. Point and laugh at the fool who says theirs is the only 'correct' way, for they are exposing the fact that they know not even step one on the path.

To differentiate between a true teacher and an imposter one must merely examine the fruit of the individual's actions. How are people around them? Are they lifted up or torn down? Energized or drained? Do they seek to empower or enslave through control. Around a spiritual person will be many smiles. Too many Ego-maniacs get a sliver of occult power and then prance around like a master wreaking havoc for themselves and those around them.

The best originator of repentance is the understanding that harming others is harming your self. We must travel back the road of our own karma to find liberation. In every situation we have been hurt, we must bring love and on every occasion where we have hurt another we must find forgiveness. Sometimes this will be between you and the individual and other times it will be between you and the Universe itself. There is a spirit within everything.

Take the Astral Shuttle to Inner Space

Anything that can be done was already intrinsic to the circumstance of life on Earth. Even enlightenment is a part of the game. Death will free you sooner or later. The longer you live to see loved ones ripped away from you, the more clearly you can hear the clock ticking for yourself.

If there is one thing that is essential to Zen, it is to keep death close. Buddha used to have his disciples hang out and watch bodies being burned. What is it that invigorates this hunk of flesh? Who is acting out this play and who pray tell is watching?

If a tree falls in the forest and nobody hears it, it still sends a wave through the air. If humanity lives and no other species in the galaxy knows it, do we still make a sound? We should be given a cosmic Oscar just for being here.

All things take place within the parameters of the Universe. When Mario dies in one of his marvelous video games, do we shed a tear or do we simply play on with another life? Eventually he makes it through and so too will we. Sinking into the moment, we find the hidden escape hatch. We can take the astral shuttle to inner space. Navigating the light filled seas, we go nowhere, anywhere, and everywhere.

We have many experiences to get the feel for every experience. Cosmic mind is the total in pure potentiality....everything that was, is, or ever shall be, existing as oneness in concept...the ability to see things from every perspective...the 'I' behind every eye. As individuals we wake into an interconnected web, working back up the manifestation chain to tune in to our soul and unite with Source.

Positive DNA Codes Bolster the Spirit

The pendulum is swinging back to center then rising once more. Indeed there are many forces at work upon the Earth. Demons, Reptilians, or just the Suppressed Subconscious; there is something dark and cloudy on our horizon. Shall we pray now for the sun? Could we even believe it if the metaphorical 'sun' were to rise and the vice-like pressure we are under as a society were to loosen? Are we going to simply give in to the shedding of rights as if it is inevitable and unavoidable?

Flood the people of a poverty stricken nation with goods instead of bombs and they will be sure to become friends. Where are we all running so fast? We need the oil to go to the job and do what? What is so gosh darn necessary? Are we accomplishing something for humanity? The details of reality are available for anybody. Our body-suits are vehicles for this 3D Earth existence. We also live in the astral realms and transcend the limitations of the doors opening outward (the senses).

It is difficult not to get worked up when you awaken to the manipulations going on all around you. Bombarded with signs, symbols, and commands, we reinforce in each other these perceptions and agree on a generally common view of reality. We can see such things as 'trees' and 'birds' and 'the sky with its clouds' and the 'starry night'. For the most part every human on Earth will have many common elements of understanding. It is about time to face that the Earth has had other children as well.

We live in a galaxy outside the bounds of our time. Remove yourself from our worldly 'advancement' and 'time period that now knows supposedly so much better than ever before' perspectives. Look outside of the impressions of history. Other civilizations from other star systems and dimensions have most certainly been around this area of space before. It is beautiful, why would they not come to visit? Saturn, its rings and moons, are known far and wide throughout the Universe.

Not all of the visitors are like the Reptilians or the Greys. Some are gentle and loving. The Arcturian, Pleiadian, and Sirian delegations have long been in support of humanity's best interest. They must get more emphasis. Yes the Reptilian entities are diabolical and relentless, but they have not the power of Love or the Joy that comes from Friendship. The Pleiadians have sent many positive codes into your consciousness. This is part of the ascension. The Arcturian contribution helps activate latent DNA that balances the aspects being turned on by messages from the controllers. Sirians give you strength and heroism...bolstering the spirit and ability to persevere.

AUM Entity Reveals Ancient Mysteries

Maturity comes when you've lived enough to get the point. It has nothing to do with paying your bills or having kids. These things are fine, but it is a perspective chiseled by time and refined by understanding that brings inner richness. Focusing on what matters most and openly declaring love for your family, friends, and fellow humanity allows the heart to share its gifts and brings to you more of the same. Taking a negative or violent approach will beget enmity and likely derail any hope you may have of awakening and realizing the full potential of your inherent nature.

At this point many people have clearly documented the territory beyond the body. There is no question about it, just whether or not the individual has found out yet. Dogma of divisiveness no longer withstands this clarity. Like cockroaches in our subconscious, they scuttle away when we shine the light of truth on them. The exclusivity of religions is the beginning of their own downfall. As if God would pick and choose among His children! Failure is a part of the game; that is why forgiveness is built into the system.

Fear and guilt are not heavenly motivators. Coming in the name of the divine, they are the antithesis of true holiness. The AUM entity is not a moralist or a purveyor of rules. AUM is the twinkle in the eye, the spice of life... Set rules for a river and it will overflow its banks. Try to coral the wind and you will get blown away. Let loose a fire and your very physical existence could be instantly incinerated. Tame the beast, but keep its spunk.

Don't look to the world for a road map to Paradise. There could not be a more confusing and contradictory set of parameters. The dog and pony show staged drama of politics is yet another splitter of mankind. C'mon, get a serious look on your face and let's talk issues. We just have to work with life as it is and everything will become clear. The only reason politics isn't a thing of the past already is because a few with diabolical self-interest intentionally keep the problems from being solved. They are well studied in pushing the mental buttons. Stepping out of the mind itself, we laugh at their puzzling expressions.

Maybe today, maybe tomorrow, but hopefully someday soon, the ancient mysteries will be commonly known. They are only a secret because a handful of gatekeepers keep them under lock and key. Some of the powers therein are indeed hot stuff and should be introduced with caution. Generally you won't assimilate more than you are able to handle. You can jump from A-Z in one leap, or you can take it slowly, drawing your letters in the sand.

We Wouldn't Have it Any Other Way

As we go through life hearkening back to days gone by and stressing over what is yet to come, we lose energy and our spirit is not in the body. We are actually astrally projecting ourselves with our attention. Longing for what isn't, we miss the gift of what is. Chaos, confusion, and eventually exhaustion are the result. Enacting causes based on false assumptions, we are surprised when we reap the effects we ourselves set forth into motion.

So often we wish things were different because we want the world to bend to our own Will. Imagine if it did! Consider what a mess we'd be in if Existence tried to follow each individual's desires simultaneously. Our whole reality would implode almost instantly. It is good that we have to plant seeds and nourish them over time. Then when our work bears fruit, we will have something of real value.

To create, we need to be persistently in the present in order to tap into the infinite reservoir of inspiration that comes from inside. Chasing our tales in the outside world with no clear vision, we dig a deeper and deeper hole. Withdrawing to the sacred place that is ours and ours alone, the million voices of advice gradually quiet and the silence gives birth to a new beginning…a rebirth that is truly our own.

Many times in Zen it is said that when the student is ready, the master will come. It doesn't always come in the form of some wise guy with a beard (although sometimes it does). Often it is the circumstance itself that we find ourselves in that is meant to elicit the response that brings us face to face with our next major challenge on the spiritual path. Wishing things were otherwise only delays our progress.

All is indeed as it should be. While we wait for aliens to save us, Armageddon to tear down the walls of oppression, or Jesus to ride in on a magic carpet, we might benefit from taking a deep breath and understanding that really there is no need. We have absolutely everything available to us here and now. In our moments of greatest enlightenment, we wouldn't have it any other way.

Alien Riff Raff and Earning your own Reward

We have everything we need for our enlightenment now. No alien landing is going to help when all the answers are already available. Metaphysically, using the great teachings of all ages, there is no obstacle to us attaining complete mastery over this realm and ourselves. It is only when we decide to put our blinders on and coalesce our Ego around a limited concept that we travel a dead end path. We have plenty of technological solutions to solve nearly every pressing worldwide issue. Humanity has not yet decided to apply these solutions, largely because political ideologies and religions still divide us down ethnic and sectarian lines.

It is unfortunate to see spiritualists putting out material that calls for people to look elsewhere for salvation. It is a harmful practice masquerading in an innocuous light. People do not need for things to be more complicated, actually quite the opposite. The simplicity of truth is its self-evidency moment to moment. There is no need for a mass influx of extra-terrestrial information. Who is to say that they would be ultimately correct anyway? Any civilization will develop and create its own idiom. Any race of beings will have their wise ones and their riff raff. Just think, can every human being be trusted? Some are brilliant and some are barely functioning.

No doubt there are star travelers that dart through our skies. What does it say for your life if you would desire them to take you away from everything that currently surrounds you? This is not a condemnation of our times but a reflection of your inability to create a circumstance in line with your heart and soul destiny. Where would these aliens take us anyway? To another planet? Why would we need this when we have a perfectly good planet of our own? The Earth has a miraculous balance of energies which spring forth life in abundance. This is rare even on a galactic scale. There is no need to beg for a pittance when we are rich with this treasure.

Lessons surround us all the time. We could learn from an alien, or we can learn from our circumstance as it stands. Other humans, animals, and our every day challenges present us with exactly what we need to take our next step forward. To long for the improbable can be an escape that delays us facing what we find in the darkest recesses of our subconscious. This is the hard work so many avoid because it is arduous and takes intense commitment and courage. If some fantastic being could magically take our pain, they wouldn't be doing us a favor. They would be rendering impossible the joy and triumph of earning your own reward.

New Transcendent Paradigm

More than ever the middle way brings to us complete relevance. The beauty of Buddha is that he is so pertinent today. "Keep death close," he might say. "Beware of extremes." That is how I like to think of him anyway. Still and happy, gentle and calm; he was a friend to all creatures great and small. Have you heard the story of Buddha having his face spit on? Buddha thanked the guy for seeing if he could still be provoked!

Reflecting everything as if you are a mirror you learn acceptance. All things are allowed in this Universe or else they wouldn't be here. Guaranteed; whatever it is that gets your goat has a lesson coded within. It is hilarious how the Universe is always trying to get our attention. This supercedes all temporal phenomena. The very fabric of space/time itself can come alive and change all the rules with a wry wink.

As the observer we are neither for nor against. Of course in the everyday world we make choices and do what we have to do, but from the eye, all simply is. Pretend to be a sacred spy with holy boots on the ground. Every dark motive transmuted by love. All offence diffused. War made into peace not anti-war. Recognize each other and work together to build the bridges that will bring the new transcendent paradigm.

From here we will be aware of all realms simultaneously and still be able to put one foot in front of the other. When we do we walk a straight path and enjoy the fruits of non-aggression. Flowers bloom around our feet as we recognize the interconnectedness of all life. Physical reality manifests around our Will as we align it with the highest truth. The divine energy comes out through our strength, sincerity and humor.

Supercede the 3rd *and* 4th Dimensions

While we enjoy the blissful ignorance of the 3rd dimension, we are surrounded by entities just out of sight on the 4th. They are an influencing factor in just about everything we do. Some stoke fears and some bring cheers, while others are just hanging around. They are often most intense at crossroad vortexes like an airport terminal or a shopping mall. They might be swirling in the air over an orchestra concert or poking their head into your bedroom through a mirror while you are sleeping. Just about anywhere there are people there are spirits.

There are angels, demons, elementals, aliens, and human souls both in and out of bodies in the 4th dimension. With just a little meditation and space from the mind, these creatures move from hypothesis to stark reality. Have no doubt they are always around. It is no harder to believe than the human beings that are living on a planet in outer space surrounded by bizarre and colorful creatures numbering in the millions. What is stranger, a grey alien that essentially shares our form, or a giraffe!?

In order to remain beyond influence, we must

be non-reactive and ever vigilant. Every impulse must be traced back to its source of origin and differentiated to glean its intent. You can isolate yourself from other humans, but it is much harder to remain free from astral persuasion. When you feel emotional pain, it draws entities that feed off of this energy. They then exacerbate the situation because their hunger is insatiable. The poor human gets caught in a downward cycle until they are destroyed and the entity moves on to its next victim.

If you are joyful and full of gratitude then you celebrate life with angels. Inviting light in, the heart opens wide and radiates a power that keeps the dark forces at bay. They will continue to send messages of deception, but if you realize where they are coming from, you can pay them no heed. Being proactive with your creativity leaves no space for the truant wanderers to occupy. As souls connected to the sun and beyond there is no astral force greater than our own if we can be resolute in our faith and adopt an unwaveringly positive attitude.

Even as we must withdraw at times from the physical world to find inner peace so too must we call our energy back from the astral. In fact we can get even more over-extended in the astral as it is much vaster than the physical and has a whole host of shifting parameters. Phasing completely into the body NOW, our soul can be HERE, and reinforce the sturdiness of our aura. The essential sacred space is your own energy field and you have every right to discretion as to what you want to let in and what you do not.

Ultimate truth supercedes all the psychodramas on any plane of existence. Those who have realized, smile because they know the freedom that comes from the cessation of all unnecessary activity. The mind will want to draw us again and again into the fray with a multitude of justifications that seem necessary. We have participated in the madness for so long that nothing going on seems almost unbearable. With practice we get used to the pleasure that stillness brings. Like a glass of water on a sunny day, we are refreshed.

2012, Awakening, and Beyond

In one sense there is nothing new under the sun. Truth is as it was and will be. There are many blossoms that represent one aspect of truth and their particular idiosyncrasies will be unique, but that is inherent in the system and nothing to get narcissistically enamored with. Right this moment you can awaken to whatever 2012 will bring and more. There may well be cosmic cycles that bring in different waves of energy, but a true seeker can rise to the ultimate heights anytime anywhere. Every moment is a call to attention. Among those of you who read this, there will be some that will not even make it to 2012. I may not live that long, one never knows. That is why 'Now' is the most crucial date.

Rather than get down by horrific happenings you can play off of them to galvanize your lucidity. If any of us live for very long we are going to be faced with things we did not want and curves in the road that we would never have suspected. Lost loves, the struggle to survive, and the quest for our own purpose are inevitable for all but the densest of rogues. Watch out for blockheads because they would rather bring down the world than open their mind. They will punish themselves until suffering ultimately confronts them to release their pride. There are many pathways out of the forest. Never let anyone convince you that there is only one. A bolt of lightning reveals the whole maze.

Collectively humanity is faced with each other and the whole of their history at once through unprecedented advancements in communication. By 2012 it should be generally easier for humanity to perceive on the 4th dimension. This is the threshold crossed as we enter the so-called Aquarian Age. At last heart wins out over mind and the wild horses are tamed. This does not mean that everyone will make it. Some will cling to the old ways, but the new generation comes of age and Love finally gets its place. Dreaming becomes another part of living and all children are taught to trust their intuition and psychic perception. The pace is slowed down and our occupations are less invasive.

From this place amidst the 4th dimension and residing on the 3rd, there is still a path to travel. 2012 will not be an end, just a noteworthy point on our journey of evolution. Obviously if so many people are drawn to wonder about this date, there is something intrinsic causing the interest. Awareness of the astral realm is something to revel in and experience in many ways. Say hi to your loved ones, angels, and colorful characters of the past. Paint landscapes of possibilities and fly toward them in your etheric body. Build a world and tear it down. Create and be like the Creator. Let the Holy Spirit move you as you dance. Laugh at the absurdity of it all then fall through space.

Some day we have to be non-attached to even our dreams. The astral realm of the 4th dimension is a continuum of vibration not a static phenomenon. Much as the ultra-violet continues out of sight, the astral realm rises up to the heavens. Observing the 3rd dimension and the 4th without judgment we carry on towards a singularity of being. This Oneness with all things is 5D enlightenment and renders all past experience into something that was meant to bring you 'Here'. Now you see yourself in everyone and everything. This brings compassion and removes violence from the equation naturally. It takes no effort to figure out it is in your best interest not to hurt yourself.

We can live in all of these dimensions simultaneously. Freedom from the mind is a must and not reacting to everything is as well. There is no way to slip through space and time if you are constantly buzzing about mundane things. The outer focus is reductive while the inner is expansive. A dispassionate look renders evenness to both realms. Fire is good but obsession can lead to ruin. Ruling out something is impossible when you realize that all things are but a subset of the possibilities. You can't deny something that isn't there in some form if only just a concept. Prepare to the point that if the whole world were to disappear you would still be simply watching and maybe even a little amused.

Together as Cosmic Mind we Travel the Universe

Looking around the world, one should not be so cynical as to suppose there is nothing good left. There are many wonderful things for which to be grateful. Having friends and hanging out on a hot summer day for instance. Being loved and loving. Hoping for a better future; this being said even amidst the backdrop of a Buddhist understanding that hope is an expectation leading to disappointment. Once you are free of the illusion, you can go ahead and hope again, not in any kind of expectation, but by radiating your light in a positive way, thereby helping to bring about the desired result. But what about, "Though shall have no desires?" Thou shall do whatever the moment calls for at once human and divine.

To the brethren and sisters I send blessings. To those dreaming of words I whisper, "Good night sleepy dreamer. One day you will awaken and when that day arrives the whole existence will celebrate." Then we can all giggle a little and rest. Tearing down is for losers and building up is for winners. Those who have mastered the fine art of bluster can point very acutely in a direction. Take a look and see what's there. Soak it up and let it pass through. If it works for you the magic will happen on its own. Beware of false idols. Neither the old man in the sky or the new age guru has the truth for you. Pilgrims don't forget about Zen. It is the invisible elephant in the astral room. It will settle things down.

Some of the information in the sources of metaphysical material is awesome, amazing, and tremendous! (Move on.) Spectacular! Preposterously enlightening!!!! (Move on.) Whatever happens…even if the Earth itself suddenly disappears, watch and maintain presence. Awareness can flow through all the realms. An Eye sees everything, and the Soul has perfect retrieval capabilities. Dig deeper and deeper still. Sometimes the way will get dark and daunting. Before you see the light, the night becomes unbearable and you find the terror that everyone is looking to stop. It must be faced inside and released in a safe manner. When we pass through it, we find true freedom, not just of body, but also of mind and soul.

Root for the home team, but always in a sporting manner. Nations are good for such things as a soccer game. Force will never be the thing to turn humanity's heart. Sometimes it is okay to let your guard down and believe in things. Sure it may disappoint or hurt you...well...believe again. Not believing in some absolute, but just the goodwill of human nature. Don't let political correctness cripple your ability to express. Sure you don't want to piss off your neighbor, but some are going to go nuts at anything you say anyway. They will be controlling you if you alter your behavior to accommodate them for fear of setting them off. It is better to be direct and kind if possible and say to them, "Stop it please".

The superstructure of emotional relationships is a human phenomenon. The sum total of all human experience is itself a conscious entity. The mood changes are the storm clouds responding to the thoughts within its mind. Sometimes it hurts itself but our love can bring it into harmony and give birth to a whole other level of sacred creature. Together as cosmic mind we will continue to travel the Universe as One (realizing Lennon's dream instead of Lenin's). In other places we can drop the seeds of our star children. Let them grow. They will struggle and face pain for there is no other way. Some will make it and some will perish for such is nature. Life is not possible if death is not on the other side.

When the End Comes Knocking on Your Door

When the end comes knocking on your door, will you be ready to greet it with open arms? Will you be able to maintain consciousness through the transition into the astral? In meditation we undergo life review before the end so that when death arrives we are clean and free to go. If we want to truly transcend this experience and get ready for departure from Spaceship Earth, we have to do soul review and release all karmas that bind us. Long lost loves and the pleasures of the garden beckon us back again and again. Just one more time in the body to dance around in the sunshine...

When the end comes will you have expressed Love fully and deeply? Will you have done the work that brought you here in the first place? Tie up the loose ends and grab your friends, we're getting the hell out of here. The forces of greed, jealousy, and pride run wild in the land of Eden. The raging dinosaurs are now out of sight, but not out of mind. Fear freezes and the enemy looks right through you. The dream of this place is more alluring than the physical reality. How it might be... Orbiting the Earth we come down for more bodies. We're rich, poor, weak, strong, happy, sad...

When the end comes will you be ready to say goodbye to everything about yourself related to the world? Your job identification, your relationship positions, and your bank account scatter to the winds. The lessons learned through life experiences remains with you. Love sustains you as you cross the threshold. When somebody you care deeply about is leaving this place, Love! "What can I do?" so many ask. Love! The sum total of our realizations will be harvested in the hours immediately after leaving the physical body behind. The lotus blossoms and magnetism draws people near.

When the end comes will your eyes be forward and not back? Can you look ahead to the adventure into the unknown? You've made the trip many times already. A remembrance and comfort will kick in and surrender will make the journey more comfortable. If you are supremely sharp you can gather your etheric body together and exit through the third eye with a dolphin dive. Swimming swiftly through the tunnel of light you can stay ahead of any dark entities trying to nip at your heels. They will be there...the many scary faces of the Bardo. Just remain focused as if you are performing.

When the end comes will it be your time, or will it come early due to negligence on your own or some other misguided soul's part? It is possible to piss the opportunity away. As long as you are alive, you can regroup and give it another go. When kids die there is usually someone else or a group of friendly entities awaiting the child's arrival. The cruelty that is possible on Earth is a remnant of an obsolete program. It is a virus that perpetuates itself. It constantly mutates and is very difficult to stop due to its supreme connivance. Fill space with light before the void gets occupied.

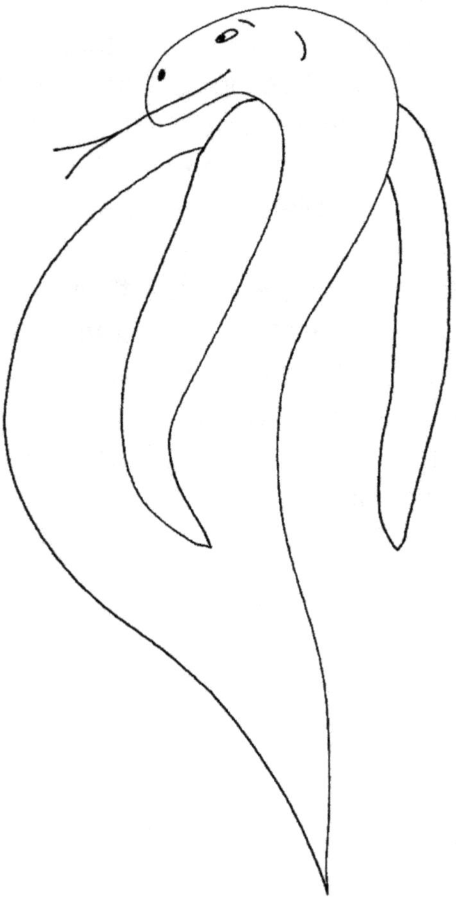

Chase out the Money Changers Again

One of the best stories in the New Testament is of a rogue Jesus chasing the money changers out of his 'father's house'. This ass kicking Jesus would likely be considered a terrorist by today's standards. The same people that pack into the churches on Sunday and consider everything said as absolute reality do not see the contradiction in their own understanding. Rather as they go about their week not worrying about their spiritual condition because it was all taken care of with their donation to the collection plate, they will likely scorn anyone who steps out of line with the matrix.

The story from the New Testament should continue from the money changer's perspective. As soon as Jesus moved on, they rushed right back in and probably cranked up their operation to unprecedented levels. Then they most likely passed some protocol that deals with preventing a circumstance like that which they just went through from ever happening again. Meet the sheeple at the door, check their IDs, and make them grovel before ever setting foot near the leaders of the status quo. Insist that they beg to be ripped off by being lent money at usurious rates.

When considering the plight of the US economy and why the squeeze is being put on the common man, it is not hard to figure out and it is not just randomly happening due to some mysterious market trends from outer space. It is completely contrived and managed to cause exactly the objective that we are now faced with. How can we not draw a direct line from the Trillion dollar wars in Afghanistan, Iraq, and the covert wars in Iran, Lebanon, and Syria to the lack of wealth within this country. Clearly it is all going elsewhere...away from the people of America.

Many researchers have already clearly demonstrated that much of the money for the wars is going to the corporations that produce the weapons and rebuild after the destruction thereby making enormous profits on both ends. Meanwhile the public is fed an endless stream of Info-tainment, and indulgences so that everyone is occupied and there is no resistance. In fact eventually the people plead for their own imprisonment in the name of security from the mysterious boogey men who seek to annihilate us. Running scared from phantoms, we are being harmed far worse!

Psychic attacks are destroying sanity and the ship of state is careening recklessly through choppy waters.

Here is a diabolical trick. Raise the price of everything through the roof and when people have no way to pay for what they've become accustomed to, hand them credit cards with interest rates up to 29.99%. Like the nation itself the individuals dig themselves in deeper and deeper just putting off the day of reckoning. Eventually everything they 'own' gets taken away and they are left on the street and actually blamed as if it is their fault for being irresponsible! The audacity of the current societal machinations is breathtaking. The country will soon share the fate of the over-extended individual.

Another nefarious plan that works really well against those who dare not think is to print money out of thin air from private banks with a name that has the word 'Federal' in it and lend it out expecting hard labor in return. What a different life for those on the other side of the printing press! Every leader who has tried to resist from a position of influence has been removed. Consider that JFK got shot just after signing executive order #11110 to return the power of printing currency back to the sovereign nation. Since then the 'Feds' have removed the gold backing of the funny money and just print it all will.

It is no surprise…in Clinton-ese…it's the money changers stupid! They ran right back into the temple (or nation) and are up to their old tricks again. Who among you is going to truly do what Jesus would do and stand up to this abomination? Reconsider your definitions and philosophies. Does it really make sense to just let these people run wild until we are all destroyed (the very thing we are afraid of and use as an excuse to acquiesce to their ambitions)? It is time to return the right of self-determination and chase the money changers back out of the temple once and for all.

The Echo of Our Own Vibration

Each moment, the actions of the present beget the future. It is not by chance that we find ourselves in any given world of time space events. We are creating it by what we choose to do and say. We are also creating it with the energy that we resonate into space from our aura. We draw to us the echo of our own vibration.

Often we see obstacles in our path that are not really there. Taking action to manifest the ideas that we have leaves the soul refreshed and with more energy to perpetuate this positive course of events. There is no greater debilitation in the Earth experience than guilt. It cripples the soul and makes magic impossible.

Freedom of motion comes from keeping a little space between our consciousness and the body. No longer bound by the rules of the physical world, a whole new series of senses comes into play. ESP, telepathy, intuition, channeling, and the creative spirit roam wild in this place. Order is a byproduct of natural expression.

Beauty is often a reflection of what one admires in oneself. At an instinctual level we find the other sex attractive. Human qualities must line up for a relationship to be successful. Sometimes for a day and sometimes for a lifetime, partners come and go with the breeze.

Patience and perseverance again and again present themselves as paths to posterity. Ask yourself, "What will I have contributed to the growth of humanity?" Just by being a good person you advance the cause of all of us. Temptation lures us astray, but through our errors we learn to walk the way.

Our Body's Life is Hanging by a Thread

To take an arrow to the heart and walk on requires patience and time. Writhing in agony, the subjected-to-the-elements divine animal scurries around. Raining pain the skies are cloudy and dark. Somehow the now self aware entity raises a fist in the air and cries, "I will survive and thrive!" Coming across another in the tribe, the conqueror is shocked when they grab an ear and whisper, "I am your enemy."

One day a friend is here and one day they are gone. Sometimes there is ebb and flow and sometimes the blow of finality. The end for each of us comes in a rush. When any two people come together, one of them will see the other dead. How do you say goodbye to a dear friend? There is no mental understanding of the disappearance from this world. There is only moving on and doing your best to live while you can.

You cannot simultaneously live in truth and falsehood. You will have to choose a path or be tormented by indecision. Then once you move, there is no looking back. All of your experiences will remain with you and you will see everyone you wish to again some day.

The big G is not cruel and is all powerful. Would your best friend leave you hanging and not let you off the hook of horror? There will come a day when we will see why.

The inner and the outer must align for peace to prevail. Too many people waste their lives following the expectations of those around them. Sometimes it is people very close to us who mislead us the most. We must have sturdiness about our own vision and walk towards our heart's goal. This is manifesting the divine will and the only real way for the mess our society is in to ever sort itself out.

We often take it for granted, but our human body's life is hanging by a thread. This world of infinite variable can throw a wild card our way at any time. What do you have left to do? If you don't feel the urgency now, wait until death strikes close to home. Then you'll know. Then you'll grow…but it won't be fun. It is however necessary. It resolves itself in the end. We will be reunited with all true loves.

We Will Die Someday Anyway

New weather catastrophes could make even the recent ones like Katrina seem small in comparison. Nukes could once again blaze in the sky making whole cities disappear in a blink of an eye. Isn't depopulation one of the fundamentals of the treaded NWO?

We could replant depleted rainforests, pass a major overhaul of animal rights, and create a health care system unparalleled in the world. We could tone down the commercials and the news realizing that kids might be in the room and consider morals a bit more important than the almighty buck.

The Galactic federation could send an envoy of Grey aliens with messages of peace and partnership. Technology could be applied universally getting all systems to operate efficiently. Food and water are made plentiful and available to all. Cameras are taken down and law enforcement becomes simple regulatory oversight. We all gain consciousness to a point where we no longer fear and realize that to help a neighbor is not a rule but in our own best interest.

The fairy realm could return and we encounter nymphs and fauns. The astral world becomes more and more visible to the average person in their daily life and they can talk to ghosts, angels, demons, gods, and goblins. We might regain our psychic powers and completely master the mind. We might even invent something new which will lift a burden from all mankind.

The Earth might get hit by a comet or go the way of Mars and dry up. We could return once more to the fate of Atlantis and sink into the ocean. All of the volcanoes could erupt simultaneously and fill the skies with smoke and burning rain. Something major happened to the dinosaurs; don't think it can't happen again. The planet could make its dreaded pole shift or be thrown out of whack by planet X. The horrible Nazis could return and finish their diabolical plans.

It doesn't matter what happens, we will die someday anyway.

A Crucifixion of Understanding

One can have something fixed in their mind and not remember the point in time when they accrued this opinion, but that does not mean that what they consider fact is correct. It very well could mean they have believed a misconception for so long that they have forgotten what it was like to live life without it. Gathering misconceptions, we build fortresses, and buttress the external lies with internal ones. Often the inner lies are the ones most difficult to see through. Admitting to yourself your own mistakes is the first and most important step on the spiritual path.

You can tell a person who is honestly doing inner work because the evolution of their being will be obviously manifesting improvements of character. Constantly watchful, every chance to heal or correct a metaphysical error is considered a blessing. Before anything else, awareness is the priority. This then makes everything illuminated with the wisdom of presence and the light of truthfulness. To misrepresent yourself is the most harmful thing you can do. What a pity people so often seek to deceive. They think that they are pulling a fast one, but the joke is on them.

When we decide to no longer sew a poor crop, we still have to reap the harvest of inconvenience that our past provides us. With patience and a focus on planting a better alternative, seasons will change and blessings will flow abundantly. There is no challenge too steep to overcome as long as you are still here. That is why it is so important not to get careless with your life. Consciously take the next step and it is much less likely that you will fall into a hole. Whether it is in this life or the next you will have to account for your choices. You might as well get it over with.

If you build a life around falsehoods it is surely as good as building a home on quicksand. It is not a question if things will fall apart, just a matter of when. There will be no way to salvation but through a crucifixion of understanding.

Distributing Healthy Lifetrons to the Earth

Sacrifice and persistence are necessary if an individual ever hopes to achieve a level of consciousness that can perceive life within and without a body. Within we see through our senses, have relationships, and contribute our talents to the world. Without, we tune into the frequencies of the astral realms, rely on our intuition, and allow creativity to move us where it will. Both are necessary to have a harmonious existence. This conundrum of balance cannot be put off. If it is not solved in this life it will have to be dealt with in the next or the next and so on.

Initially most throw themselves into the world and focus on careers and family. After a time many feel called to introspection and reevaluation of their methods. Seeking a higher power they begin to release Ego's mighty grip and see that they are a part of a grand schema. Enemies and friends alike serve as reminders to awareness and self-control is found as the key to personal freedom. Calmness sets in and space allows for everything to blossom in its own time. Passion can burn hot and without proper channeling it will inevitably be a destructive force.

Each will find a different path that leads them forward. There are no two human beings alike in their makeup. Some have similarities and will thus be draw to like-minded circumstances, but the road home will diverge and the glory of salvation will be yours and yours alone. This is why no one religion can ever suffice for humanity. In fact 300 hundred will not do the job. 6.5 billion composites of the world's wisdom are needed for the 6.5 billion unique expressions of the source. Anyone who preaches in absolutes and exclusivity is trapped in a mental faux pas no matter what their claimed intention.

Our population is rising quickly because souls are becoming increasingly fragmented. Instead of one soul for one body, shattered souls take several bodies at once. They will eventually have to work their way back to unification as a soul and then they can concern themselves with unification with source. Too often they run blindly through the world slamming into walls and magnifying their karma instead of transmuting it. Eventually there is a point of no return if it goes on long enough and the energy instead of coagulating disperses. New forms may emerge one day but the difference will be such that the original light of manifestation will no longer be recognizable.

Discipline imposed from without, no matter how firm and appropriately conceived cannot do the job of corralling these intense forces. The discipline must be of the self and enacted because the individual sees the sense in it and feels aligned with this undertaking in their heart. Love is the glue that holds the Universe together. Many have stumbled upon this truth, but the multi-faceted meanings can still remain elusive. It is not just the extremes of the 60's peace movement approach. It is often doing the difficult things that keep people from harm. Sometimes we must overturn the applecart full of rotten apples in order to harvest a fresh batch and distribute healthy lifetrons to the Earth.

Promised Land Within

To begin pontificating, one must assume that there is something worthwhile to convey. How is this value attained? One soaks up information, transcends it, and then uses it to describe their experience. Some people are naturals in a given arena while many have a hard time finding their right place in the world. Hardship bypasses one group of people and visits another. The rollercoaster of life keeps bringing all of us up and down. The mass media blitz immerses us in subconscious commands. Talking mouths are yap yap yapping at us from every direction. Where can we go to get a break from the madness?

If we take a trip to the mountains and our mind is still stressed, we have not really gotten any space between our center and that which ails us. Unplugging from the network both technologically and sociologically is an important skill which is too often neglected. We have to know a part of ourselves that is not related to the outside. Comparison, conclusion, and confusion need not approach. Trust, acceptance, and courage make possible the survival of the gap in order to reach the promised land of heaven within.

You will be God's chosen person; you will see that this was inherent from creation.

It is not possible to sustain borrowing from tomorrow to pay for today. At some point you'll have to work two or three times harder just to break even. It is better to work now and get over the hump. Not putting off until tomorrow what could be done today is a Franklin aphorism worth remembering. In his autobiography are many gems of simple living. Best of all, he was not a fanatic. Most of the founding fathers of America had a true mystical sense of religion. They didn't believe in formulas but in human divinity. They were carrying on a tradition at least as old as Ancient Egypt and perhaps Atlantis.

Neutral observation is the master key. Judgment begets association. Awareness sees without reacting. If necessary in the moment action will take place. Learning the mechanisms of the body/sensory apparatus, we can essentially slip out of it. The real happenings occur in the loose space behind bodies. Here is a whole other sub-stratum of existence. Many subtler shades of entity will be interacting with you. You must learn to watch that too. Some of us are known for our inter-dimensional travel abilities. It is inwards that we fly. Not just in a concept but as a launching point for greater journeys.

We are human fish in a cosmic pond. Swimming through space, we learn lessons under the watchful eye of Father Zeus. Breathed by the force which pervades all, we mistakenly believe we are separate beings: temporary differential patterns clinging to form in an ever transient flow of change. Soon the waves in the sea will wave goodbye to the current hunk of flesh. When they do, what will remain? Their etheric double will hang around for awhile, then to life review and the portal to incarnation. If you have gained a good amount of momentum, you can fly up to the higher astral and chill.

A Flame Lives Strong in the Heart

Is it not a wonder to realize that there are mammals in the sea that are rather quite intelligent and even friendly in their general demeanor? Many angelic beings take dolphin form when incarnating on the Earth. Just as with humans, some of them are celestial and some of them are not. The determining factor is the soul quality.

This is a terrifying place and that more than anything is why we forget. Seek continuity and the string that runs through your existence will reveal all. Weep not tears for pain gone by; there is plenty more to come. Life can too often turn to tragedy. This is an expression of the karmic debt of all of humanity. Much has been denied.

Do you think Earth could not bring back her Thunder Lizards if she chose too? It is only the benevolence of the gods that keeps humanity around a bit longer somewhat for their amusement and to give us yet another chance to get things right. Constantly moments slip away and the heart cries while the mourners tear out their hair.

The body is the vessel for the traveling soul. You can move into any form if you are aware enough to remain conscious through the death portal. You should be able to jump anywhere in the timeline. Often it is baser instincts that drive the incarnation. Diving quickly into the next body available, souls miss the chance to refine.

Try not to be lulled into a false complacency that allows you to put off the pressing business of self transformation. The work is hard and the time is short. Your worldly pursuits make way for inner sensibilities. Whatever direction the collective shall move, the individual can maintain another. A flame lives strong in the heart.

Witness the Stupendous with Understanding

Every second of every day you are praying. The thoughts in your head, your emotional state, and the quality of your heart send a resonance out into the infinite that bounces back in kind. There is not a thing put before you that hasn't somehow been long in the works. One gets discipline when they learn it is in their own best interest.

Osho said that when you harm another first you must harm yourself. One of the most important practices to undertake is that of being non-reactive. Most of the ills in the world come from a chain reaction of events one begetting the other. That is the deeper meaning of Jesus' turn the other cheek. Someone has to break the cycle.

If you believe yourself to be of a spiritual nature then the onus is on you to be the difference maker. Many people are oblivious to the currents of energy that flows all around and through us. It is up to us to ground the energy and live the example that others can see. The more difficult the situation, the more important the practice.

It is easy to surround yourself with those of like mind and continue to reinforce in each other your predispositions. Beware! This is incredibly dangerous if your true goal is self-realization. Many get so blown away by their early psychic perceptions that they think they have already arrived. The Tao winds on even if you decide to stop.

Often the subtle is far more effective a witnessing to the stupendous than the overt. Shout to someone who is not quite ready and they might run or worse close their doors to the magnificent. Being kind, making friends, and speaking in a language that others can understand will far more likely achieve the desired results of the Lord's work.

Apocalyptic Dreams and Universal Love

When the echo of life begins to ebb, will you still be able to flow? Has the world beaten you or have you risen to the challenge? Many things happen on the outside that seem to be uncontrollable but which actually are a reflection of the seeds we have planted long ago and are only now just harvesting. With the imposition of Will, a difference can truly be made. Pool energy and focus intensely on a goal. Dispersion of attention is a great weakness.

Pyramids are power because they focus energy. We can focus our own energy and as the creator build mental bridges in service of our own goals. When we align our own values with the laws of the Universe, the resistance will be minimal. Even with all the chaos going on in the land of Eden, you can manifest an oasis of abundance. It may well take a lot of work. Turning stress/strain into strength is the key to perseverance through difficulties.

Human beings have tremendous potential. Shine with brightness amidst the confusion. It can not be other than that your attitude will be rewarded. We need not be ultimately perfect though we try with our whole heart. This is understood and is not a disqualifier to the cause of good. Sometimes we begrudge our brethren, when with a little compassion/empathy we can understand more deeply and meet them where they are comfortable.

Humanity socially has gone quite off the deep end as of late. There is a turning of the screws that everybody can feel. Sometimes it hits really close to home and sometimes it hits YOU. There is no reason that people should be in this position at this point in our development. The solutions to every problem are readily available. They are not manifested because of groups fighting with each other over money, a non-existential thing.

We may not always get along, but let us appreciate each other while we can. Everybody has something unique to contribute or they wouldn't be here. There is no thing in this Existence which is coincidental. All is accounted for and permeated with consciousness. Sometimes the master plan seems to go off the charts but if you look closer it never really goes all the way. People scare themselves with apocalyptic dreams, while the Universe loves.

It All Resolves in the End

On a Sphere in Outer Space, we have expelled ourselves from the Kingdom of God. Cut off in the Mind by the Powers, we are hardwired into the Network. Through the eyes dear, through the eyes...

A Field of Foolishness; baseness and purity collide to make a Mush of Morals. Like the Knights of Old, some spit into the wind and then duck just before Karma calls. Through the ears dear...through the ears...

One day dug deep into the dirt, we will leave the body to the worms and the dust. The Sun will still Rise and the Son will still surprise. The Moon provides better cover for Lovers. Through the fears dear, through the fears...

Talking faces speak feces with ease. They like war and suffering. Energized the most when pain is acute, the flames are fanned and shock is feigned when the obvious occurs. Too proud to repent. Through the tears dear, through the tears...

Walking over the edge, unknowing takes hold and cleanses the soul with distinct sharpness. Suffering was but the means to the end of the world. This does not end Life, just Death.

There is not a date of doom, only Time. Through the years dear, through the years…

Species have come and gone with humanity soon to follow unless they seed Venus with their DNA. One need not wonder why the bugs and the dinosaurs relinquished their dominion over the planet. They were forced to by circumstance. Rest not easy. They both seek to take back what they believe to be theirs. Through the aeons dear, through the aeons…

The Egyptians still fight with the Kabbalists while the Christians and Muslims poke each other in the eye. Buddhists bite the master's finger and Hindus float in the sky. Respect the traditions as a scholar and remove the obstacle they create in the path of the moment. When the Gates are open, we will see it is not what it seemed to be. Throughout eternity my dear, throughout eternity…

There are creatures above and below. Reach high and when ghouls seek to grab you by the foot, shine brightly and strongly say, "NO!" Guilt will follow and when it does, strike with the Sword of Wisdom. Burst energy through your Aura and let the Force take its course enlivening and enlightening. You are the

Raison d'être of the whole Universe. It all resolves in the end my dear, it all resolves in the end.

Every Waking Moment

The scourge of humanity is Guilt, and those who perpetuate it are the enemies of Heaven. God is blamed when it is the lack of our Compassion for each other that causes Strife. The Greeks anthropomorphized many forces of Nature and they were not wrong. We have lost many of the ancient mysteries and mistakenly scoff when Wisdom is staring right at us.

There are vibratory realms above and below the frequencies we exist within. There are small creatures and large with a zillion permutations bringing endless fascination. The line of Time misleads as everything happens at once. It is terrifying how magnificent it all is. Evolution is but a swirl on the canvas. Boost thought capacity to grand scales without borders.

Karma is like an invisible rubber band bouncing your every radiance back to you. It is the ultimate neutral teacher. As Barry Long explains we are actually praying always. When Christians say God knows every thought it is essentially the truth. Everything is on display. We are naked with our clothes on. Like little larvae we play with our toys and cry over spilt milk.

When we raise our hands to the sky the Spirit will rain down on us. As long as we keep our eyes towards the ground we remain in Hell. Constantly trapping each other
in confusion, the blind lead the blind over the cliff. In the instant before Death it occurs how precious Life truly is/was but at this point it is too late. That knife's edge Consciousness has to be there every waking moment.

The Most Precious Gift of Life

Neutral observation is the cosmic loophole which frees us from the chain reaction of cause and effect that echoes through generations. Turning the other cheek is the spiritual way to stop evil in its tracks. If you return a blow with a blow there will undoubtedly be yet another blow soon to follow. Imagine thousands of these events occurring on and on. Not hard to do as we are immersed in this very circumstance.

How mortally offended we get over the smallest affront to our sense of self importance! See without motion; make it a cultivated habit to wait. Often we will be convinced that action is immediately necessary, but this is rarely the case. Perhaps in an emergency quickness is needed, otherwise the only hurry is a self-imposed one. Many problems will instantly dissolve when they are not created in the first place.

Hear what the other is saying from their perspective without projecting preconceived judgments. You will make many friends by listening with an open mind. It is a kind of violence to seize upon another's words/world and try to force it into your own. The Universe has infinite space for any possibility to occur. If something is expressed, it had to have prior existence in the ether in order to be revealed.

We take things too seriously down here on Earth. Tension creeps in and we forget to laugh. Tricksters breach our trust and then it becomes difficult to trust again. It is up to a strong heart and an aware consciousness to understand these idiosyncrasies and continue to love. Vulnerability is possible only in naivety. If we know that a particular behavior is an inherent part of the game we can not be hurt by it.

We are all children of God; it couldn't be otherwise. Any who declare exclusivity are delusional. It is like siblings constantly fighting over whom daddy or mommy likes best. Each child sees their parents differently and it stands to reason that there will be as many perceptions of God as there are people on the planet. We may sometimes feel frustrated but already have the most precious gift of life.

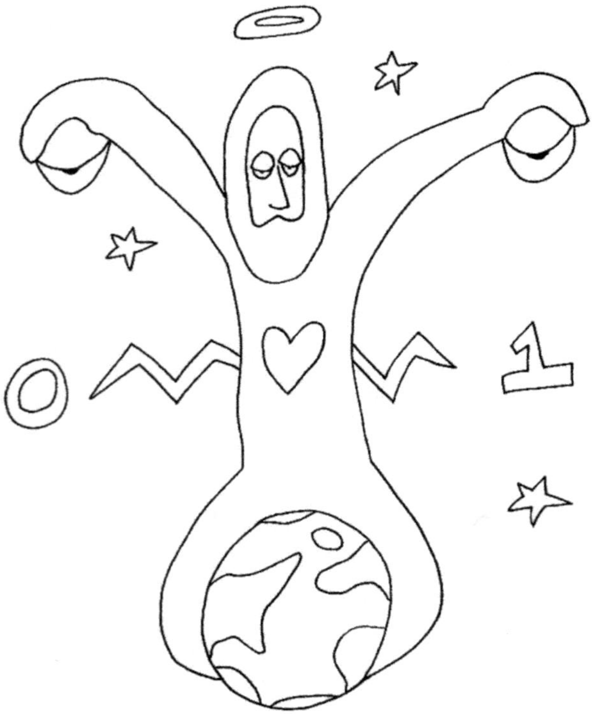
0
1

Single Flames must Shine Bright

The absurdity of reality begets the unusual. As much as we'd like to hold on to our illusions, they evaporate with the changing of the season. Random variables happen across our path attracted by the unfinished business of the subconscious. This can manifest in a myriad of ways. It draws in both the good and the bad…that is until it all becomes pure experience. It isn't about trying to superimpose upon what is, it is accepting what is and joining your voice to the chorus.

It is sorrowful to isolate yourself and judge against the inevitable. People have to learn through their mistakes. They try on many masks and dance the dance of seven veils. All the while the heart aches to be together, throbbing on the most basic level of love. The world is meant to be difficult and the trials give us strength. Loss helps us appreciate and friendship makes us whole. Things don't have to be perfect. An understanding that we are in the same boat often helps.

Being coaxed out, we should turn in. The freedom we seek is detachment from the chaos. Contradictions, hypocrisy, and denial are presented as normal and the resulting insanity is treated with meds. Anything goes and culture is reduced to the lowest common denominator. Single flames must shine bright to illuminate the potential. There are many counter-streams to this subterfuge. One Will can turn the tide for the whole planet. Begin again and again.

Gateway to Another World

Warbling like a nightingale, the stream of imagination-trons dives into 3D and animates physicality. Coaxing the tune from the Source with a smile the Spirit babbles down the hill of frequency. Like a cosmic xylophone the melody is clunked out with humor and style.

It is a dangerous place, this forest/jungle. There are many creatures lurking in the night. Fear is in the air and it is not without some justification. Something does go BUMP in the night! The black hole of national debt seeks to engulf all of us. We need to be like Mario and solve the puzzle.

Our Ship of State is rocking upon the waters. The USA has to print its own money and set up programs to pay off high interest loans with low interest loans. There is nothing more compassionate than to save the populace from the crime of Usury. A refocusing on the divine humanity that has been the goal of every great civilization would help as well.

There needs to be more general spirituality centers in this fruited land. If we are truly going down the road of multi-cultural society, integration lies in non-exclusivity. A rose by any other name smells just as sweet and the Holy Spirit wearing any disguise is just as gloriously magnificent. We are given a small pocket of time to express the inexpressible at the discretion of the Creator.

You may sometimes ask. “Where is God in all of this mess?” In every kind gesture, every friendship, and every sunrise the presence of the Universal Consciousness is there. It comes from another place and manifests in the form of the circumstance. It is hard to explain how in one second every wrong can be made right, but it is so. The ‘moment’ is not just a psychological practice it is a gateway to another world.

A Dawning that Surrounds Us

If you think that you will never love again, even a slight opening left in your heart will allow that which is beyond you to save you. It is a power surpassing all others, within every atom of existence. If you ask, "Of what stuff is heaven made?" Love would be your answer. It is not a Love of limited definition. It is a dawning that surrounds us.

Enjoy the precious moments of Life. There is an inevitability of inconvenience and hardship to overcome when you incarnate on this planet. When you have a special occasion, relish it! There is no greater luxury than being alive. Simple connections nourish the soul. Remember the amazing circumstance and be grateful for the opportunity.

There is quick attractive response when intention is pure/clear. Sometimes a little patience is necessary. Moaning and groaning never helps. Fixing firm on the positive brings about the best results. The change that people seek is the one only they can provide: a synergy of strength, intelligence, kindness, imagination, and compassion.

Self-Deception: Scourge of Humanity

What makes even the weakest simpleton dangerous? When they believe themselves to be correct! There are millions of little experts running around out there commenting on millions of things that they have no idea about. It would be hilarious if it wasn't so deadly. The protection of Denial becomes the most important underlying factor in their lives because otherwise they couldn't take the next step forward.

If you are then to engage one of these absolutely correct individuals in conversation and question the veracity of their arguments, brace yourself for what is to occur next. Likely they will search your entire subconscious for the thing that will hurt you the most and attempt to go there. Very likely they will try to turn the conversation around and make it about you. They will howl and wail, but you must hold strong.

Nobody is required to live in an abusive environment. Problem is that these days it is hard to find an atmosphere including humans that isn't poisoned with the symptoms of the crumbling values in our society. Christianity is falling but that doesn't mean the other religions are correct. The essence that gave rise to the old religions and many more lives still and it is through this Source vibration that we will find salvation.

Over many years of being beat down, a person gets cut off from pieces of their being. Whatever wasn't allowed a true and full expression remains in Space waiting for the day it can return to the whole soul. Before these missing pieces are reclaimed, little progress is possible because the unresolved feelings will constantly hinder all subsequent relations. It is through healing that our energy centers can awaken.

Key to the whole process is expression. When the backlog is processed and expunged, then the greater lessons of your soul can be assimilated. You're not here to just piddle around with your local circumstance. More than anything you are given the opportunity to find the jewel within. Even right now it is shining. The song goes on and at any point you can clear the air, free the mind, and join in.

Soul and its Influencers

Angels and Demons are Souls without a body. We are Souls within a body on this continuum of Good to Evil. The discarnate speak to us as do the embodied. Messages bombard from every direction. Command and control is the name of the outer game. Freedom cannot be obtained without until it is secured within. Fear is only possible when you do not have the inner connection which transcends individual permutation.

The specificity of your place on the A-D scale lies in the aura's vibration resonance. It is your pitch; the sound of your hand clapping. There are many beings in the dreamlike place beyond the body constantly moving into our space. Unless hip to their existence, people will feel the entities influence as if it is their own conception. This is one of the things that make the unholy influencers so dangerous. They prey upon the weak.

The old world passeth away and the whole history of humanity happens again in a huge flash before disappearing completely. A societal life review sets us all up for the next adventure. The internet has caused a kind of madness. We are losing touch with nature and the reality of the seasons. Planet Earth groans under the weight of Her children and their inventions. They pierce her skin and she is bleeding to death.

Naked leaders parade around in suits and ties. They make decisions for everybody based on their own best interests not those of the community. It is simple decency that is missing; a hand-shake deal or a word that can be trusted. The rulers of the day do unto others the most horrible of things. They must follow Satan. Ye shall know them by their fruits. Do they bring forth nourishing food, or does it stink like a rotting corpse?

These words exist merely in the metaphysical. They do not mean a thing that you are not applying to it. A bit of common ground we share, so I can encode an S.O.S. from you to you. Some of us are able to reflect the truth of the Soul. This does not always feel good, but it does end well. The same old same old is not going to do anymore. A certain amount of force is going to have to be applied to stop the bleeding…a Soul tourniquet.

The Echo Rings Throughout Eternity

The mysteries of this existence are many. Right down to the very atoms that reside in space, this illustrious illusion continues to convince us of its reality. This creation we reside in is a meeting ground for us to share experiences. Even as a dream we must inhabit an environment in order for something to take place within it.

All around us are the eyes of God (animals) and the eyes of the state (video cameras). Which ones do you want to poke out? How has everything gotten so backwards? Denial has been impressed in a big way and the stakes have grown extremely high. To release this pressure, somehow it must be directed in a safe way.

One terrible option would be a war far worse than any we have seen. Quick and devastating, like Einstein's prediction, we will have destroyed much good with the bad. Would it not be better to be analytical, rational, and reasonable in our deliberations? Empirical facts can bring real results.

From nothing we come and to nothing we go. The echo of what comes in between rings throughout eternity.

Sublime Times of Transcendent Joy

Beautiful things happen when you are patient and do good works. Blessings follow a truthful heart. If you cannot find what you seek, leave the door open for it to find you. The magic of life is beyond what our mind might preconceive. Accept things when they are offered freely and share in return. Gifts shower upon those who love.

It is a service to receive in a healthy way. This enables others the fulfillment that comes with giving. Too often we look to the horizon for a fleeting image of lasting happiness, when the secret is right in front of us. Even when the world is falling apart, one wonderful moment supersedes the chaos and the purpose of being here is realized.

Adversity presents itself in many forms. Sometimes we feel pinned in and our inner juice is all but used up. It might take a great revolution of the spirit to change the circumstance. If the potential for awakening your deeper truth is at stake, it is usually worth it to take the risk. Rejuvenation is an ongoing process that will heal.

Sublime times of transcendent joy are why we come here. To swim upstream is the song of Tao. The contrast is made so the illusion can become manifest. Past the two
is the infinite and from here
comes eternal truth at once; cosmic mind in all possibility before it plays out. The Big Bang is still happening. It's just been a split second.

You Can Never Die When You are Loved

From inner space to cyberspace while we all float in outer space, higher dimensional frequencies surround us. We are immersed in a complex grid of communication with messages from many sources seeking to reach us and influence our actions. Propaganda from the astral realm is a big threat to our individual sovereignty. Indirectly it flows from demons to boardrooms to television sets; directly it flows right into any crevice of our being that is not illuminated with the presence of soul.

There are many positive intentions floating around out there and if we choose carefully, they can assist us in our own transformation as divine beings. How can we tell if a message is malignant or benign? The first second's intuitive reaction reveals whether any given information is helpful or hurtful. As soon as the feeling goes into rationalization, we are lost in the maze of our preconceptions. There is no need to hold onto a truthful tapestry of meaning as revelation occurs on its own.

We can take actions to create a better world, but if they are unconsciously influenced by subtle nefarious undercurrents, we may well be adding to the confusion. Perhaps the best thing we can do is radiate goodness in our daily lives. Any time we are helpful towards our fellow humans or kind to nature itself, we can be sure we are on a straight path. Encountering what is in front of us with awareness, dark energies retreat and a serene calmness smoothes over angular discrepancies.

Life on Earth is an opportunity, not a guarantee. We have to walk/talk thoughtfully and consider our moves carefully. There is no need to rush as we may miss the moment. It is essential to make the most of this rarest of miracles and extract everything we can. We take for granted the obvious because as far as we know it has always been the case. Imagine the journey your soul must have taken to find a body and then be consciously in the driver's seat. How could it be? But it is!

When the weight of the world is weighing heavily upon your shoulders and that brow of yours is getting furrowed, remember that one day you will slip out of this physical existence and leave all encumbrances behind. Pressures are only as important as the credence you give to them. Love now, and let the rest fall where it will. In times of crisis we get the clarity to see what is truly important. With wisdom we do not need a calamity to have the same vision. Everything is laid bare and we see.

Delight in the simple pleasures of being here. Watch the sunrise, hold somebody's hand, and say what is in your heart. You can sit around complaining about what you do not have, or take joy in what you do. In this way, we create our own reality and draw to us more of what we are resonating. Life is a blank canvas and our every day environment provides plenty of colors to paint with. When you are gone from this place, leave friendship in your wake. You can never die when you are loved.

Also by Christopher Moors

Rainbow Sky

Enchanting tales that would entertain even the hardest of hearts. Have tea with Bigfoot and the Loch Ness Monster, learn what the animals say and oodles more.

Pearly Gates Press

Take a journey through the astral realms. Awaken the truth encoded deep within your DNA. Open up to a cosmology you always hoped could be.

Ruminations of the Universe

Enlightenment, Transcendence, and Super Channeling, in a book that will open your eyes and shed light onto the mysteries hidden just behind the veil of illusion.

Mission of the Creative Cosmos

To invoke the unity of Eastern Wisdom and Western Art.

To assist in the evolving consciousness and destiny of humanity.

To make this information available to the widest possible audience.

http://www.creativecosmos.org

www.ingramcontent.com/pod-product-compliance
Lightning Source LLC
Chambersburg PA
CBHW051839090426
42736CB00011B/1880
* 9 7 8 0 9 8 5 6 9 7 9 3 8 *